"The pessimist sees difficulty in every opportunity. The optimist sees opportunity in every difficulty." — Winston Churchill

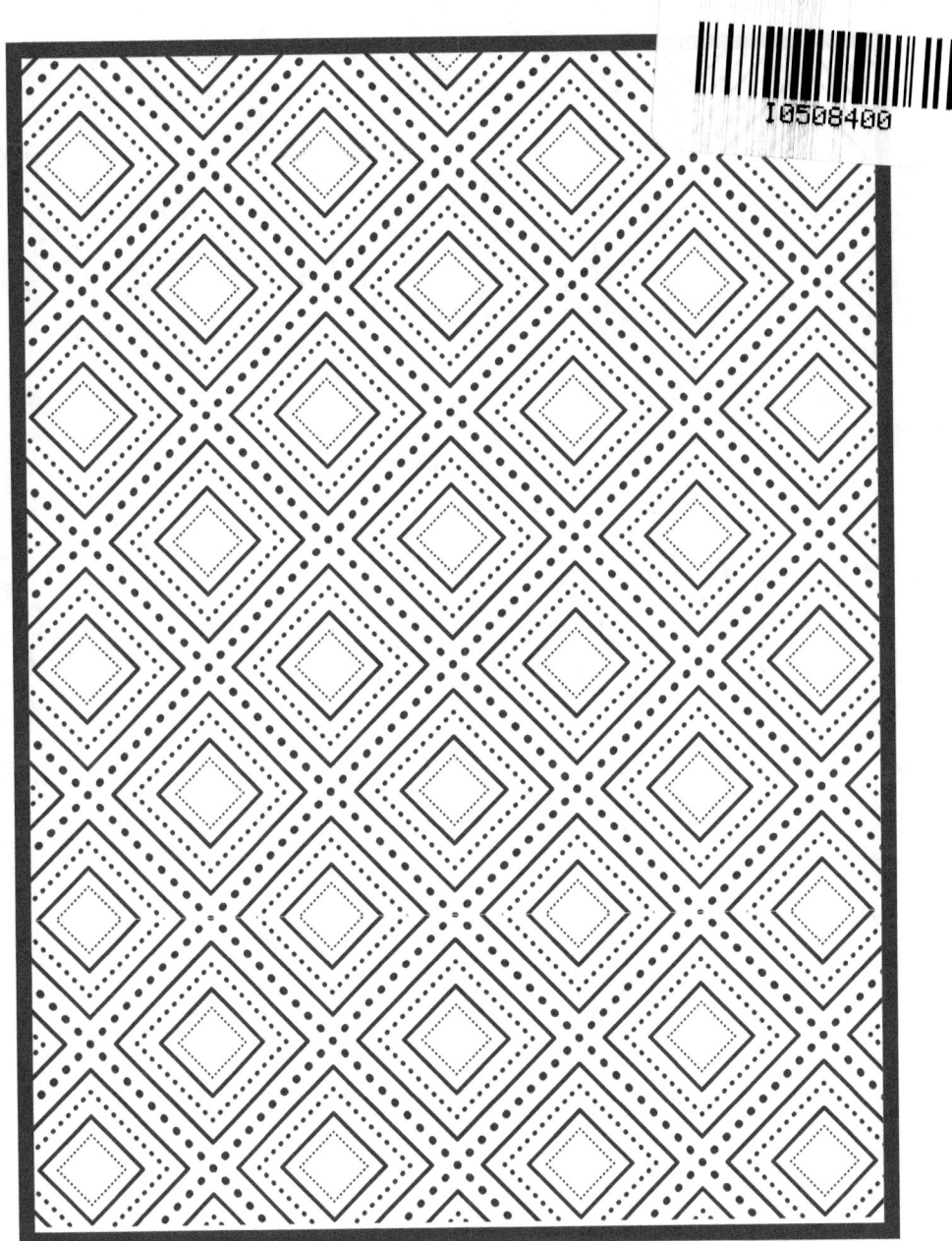

"Don't let yesterday take up too much of today." — Will Rogers

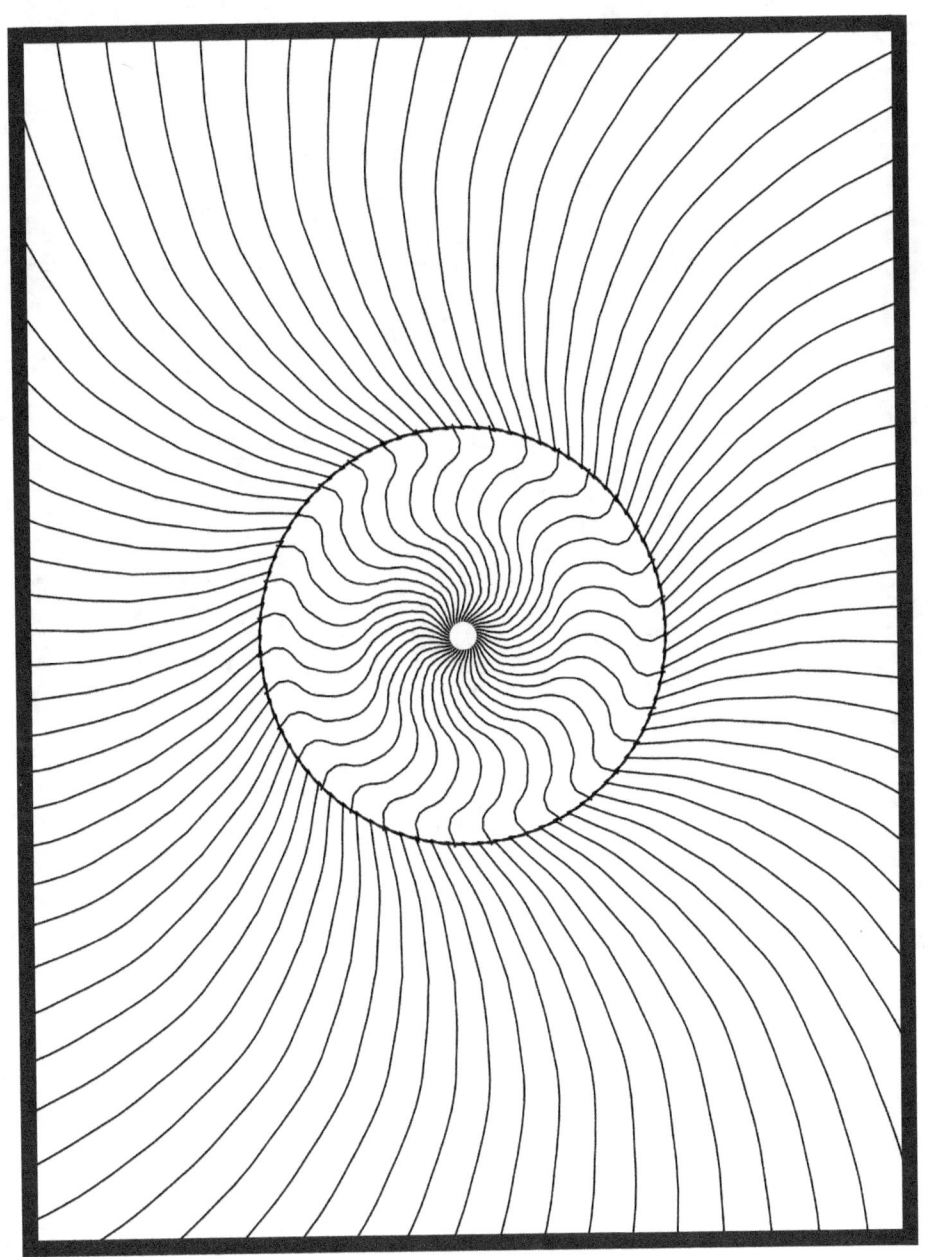

"You learn more from failure than from success. Don't let it stop you. Failure builds character." — Unknown

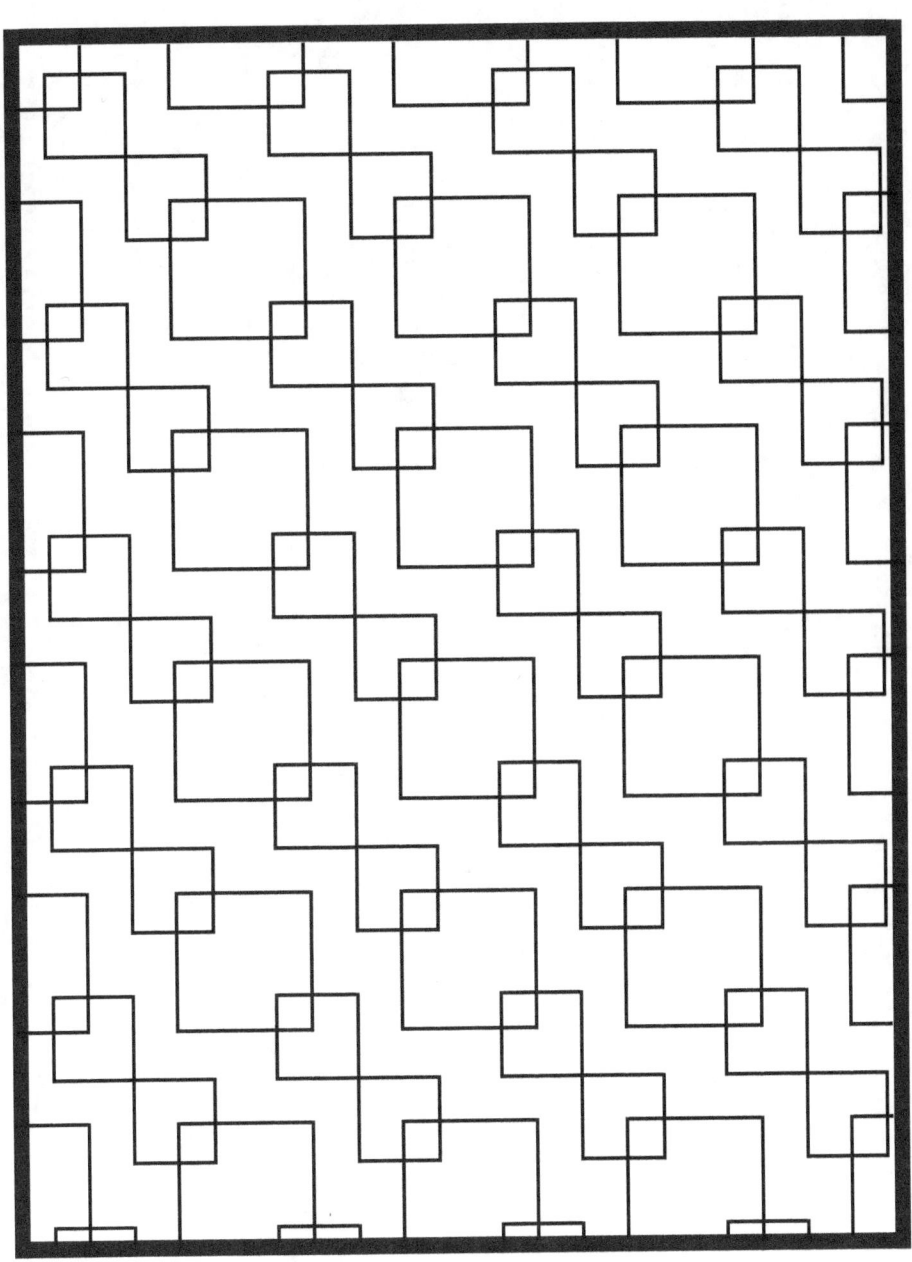

"If you are working on something that you really care about, you don't have to be pushed. The vision pulls you." — Steve Jobs

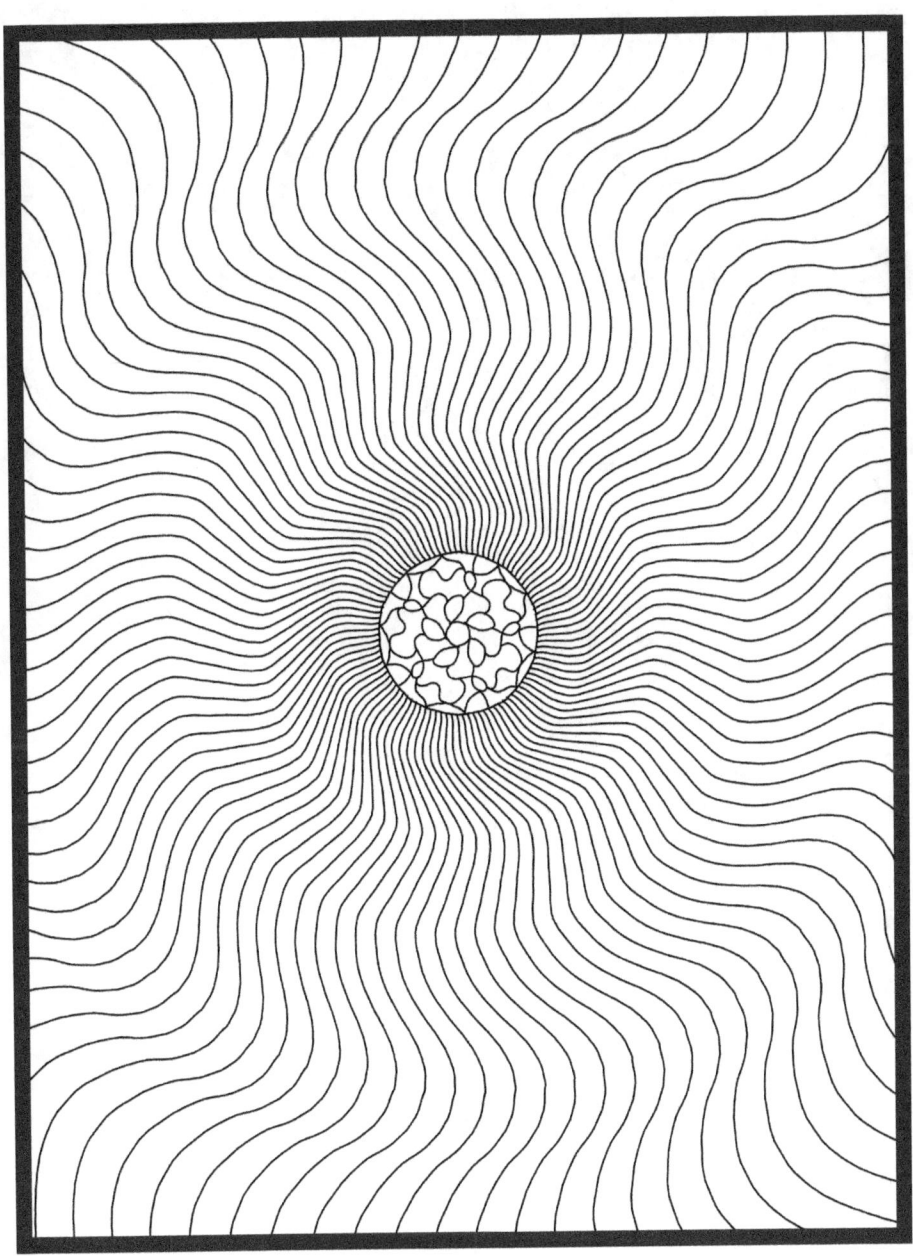

"Experience is a hard teacher because she gives the test first, the lesson afterward."
—Vernon Sanders Law

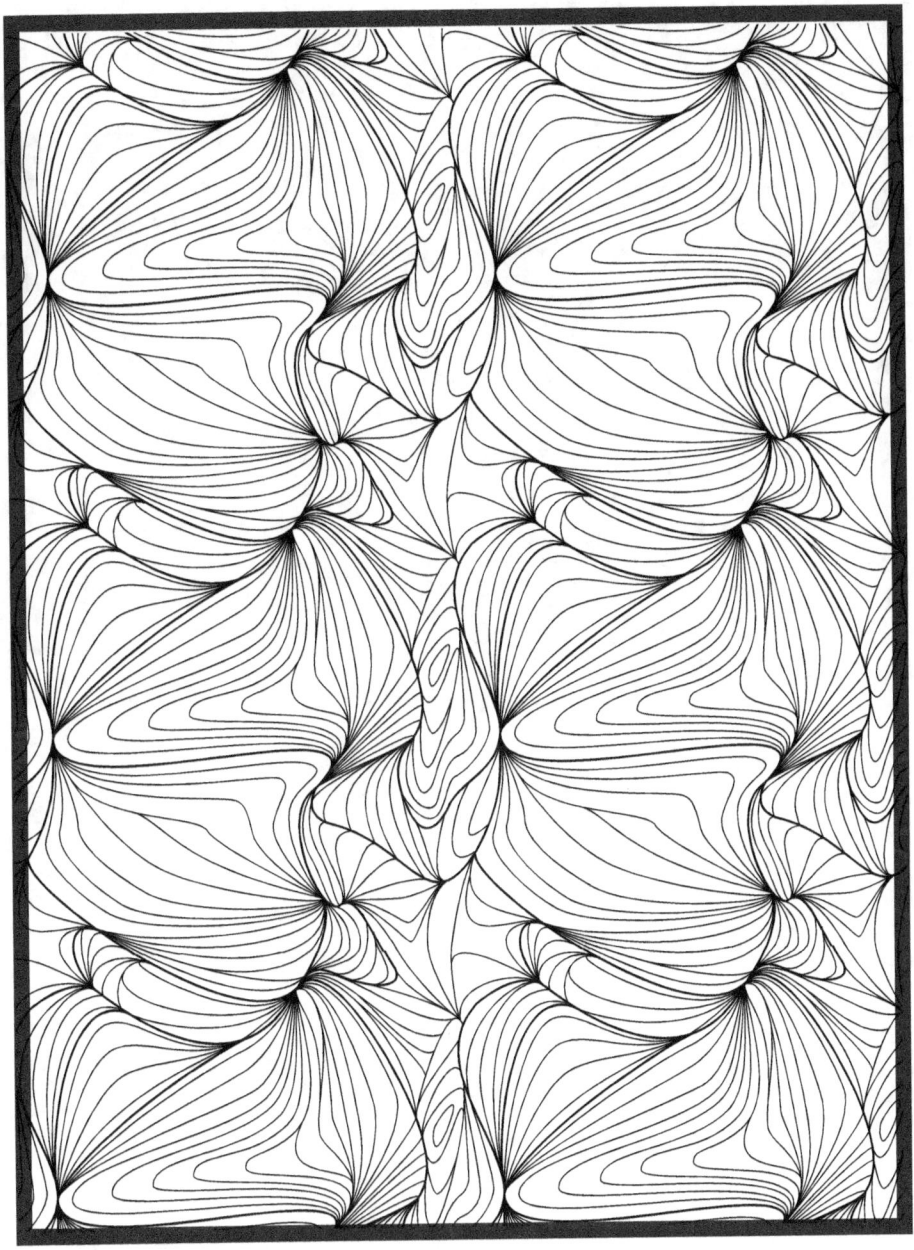

"To know how much there is to know is the beginning of learning to live." —Dorothy West

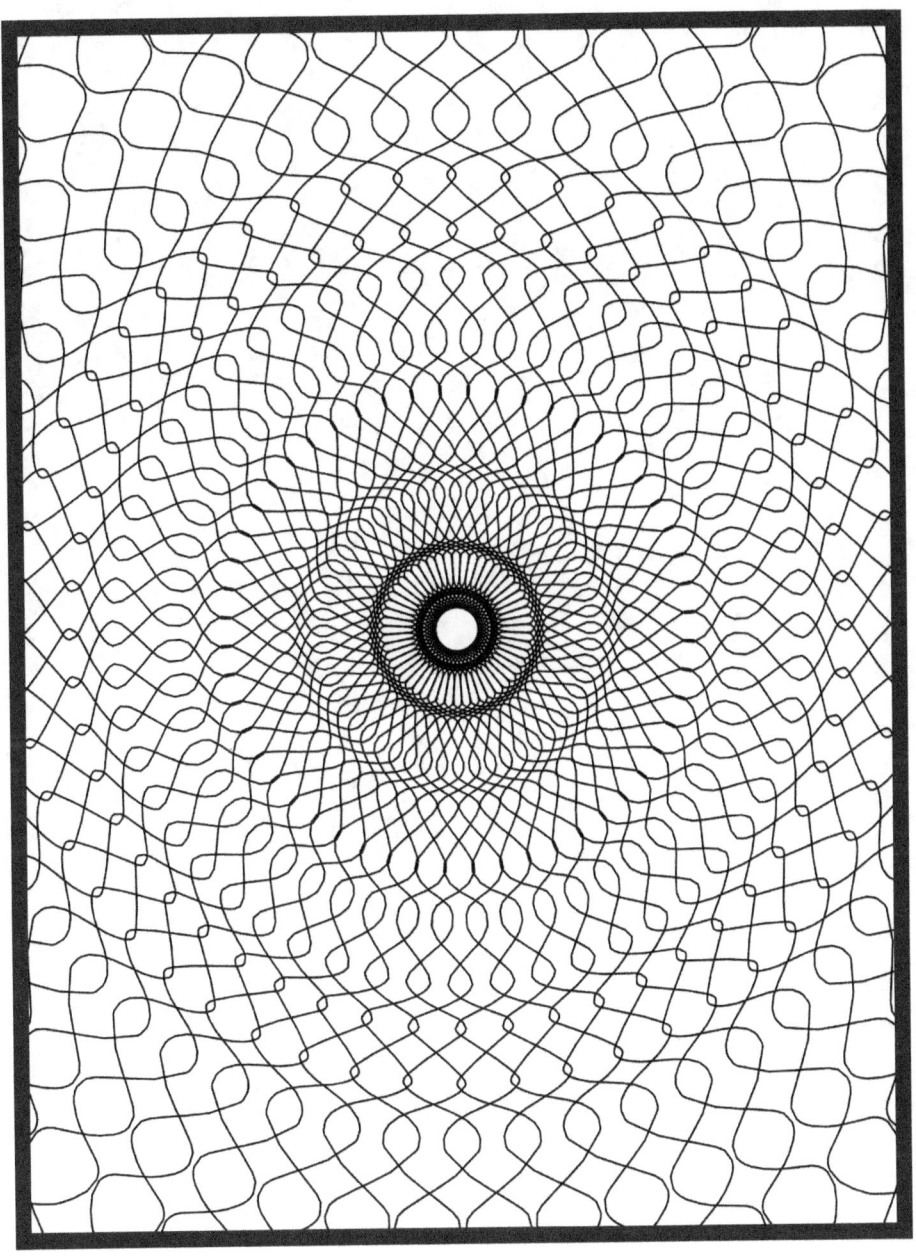

"Goal setting is the secret to a compelling future." — Tony Robbins

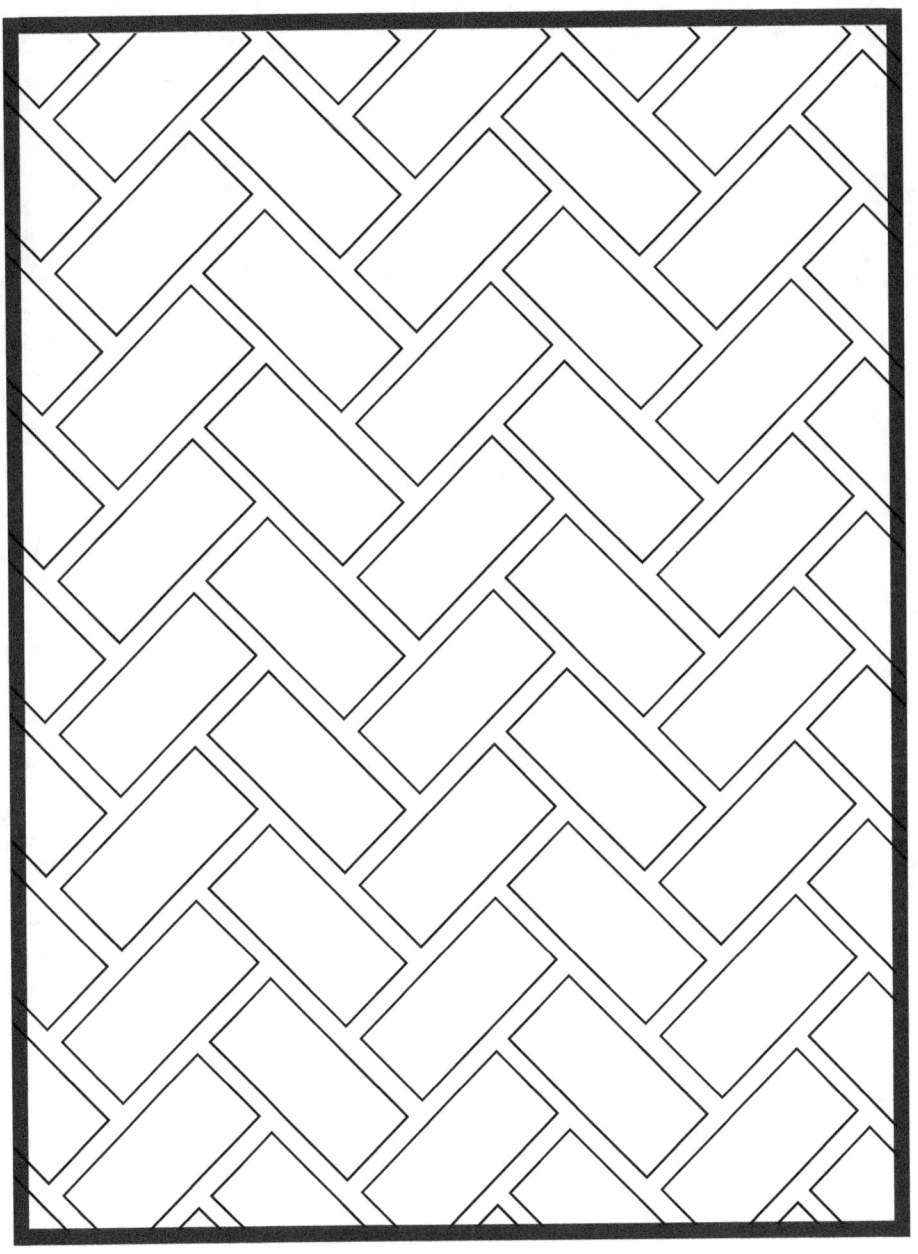

"The elevator to success is out of order. You'll have to use the stairs, one step at a time." — Joe Girard

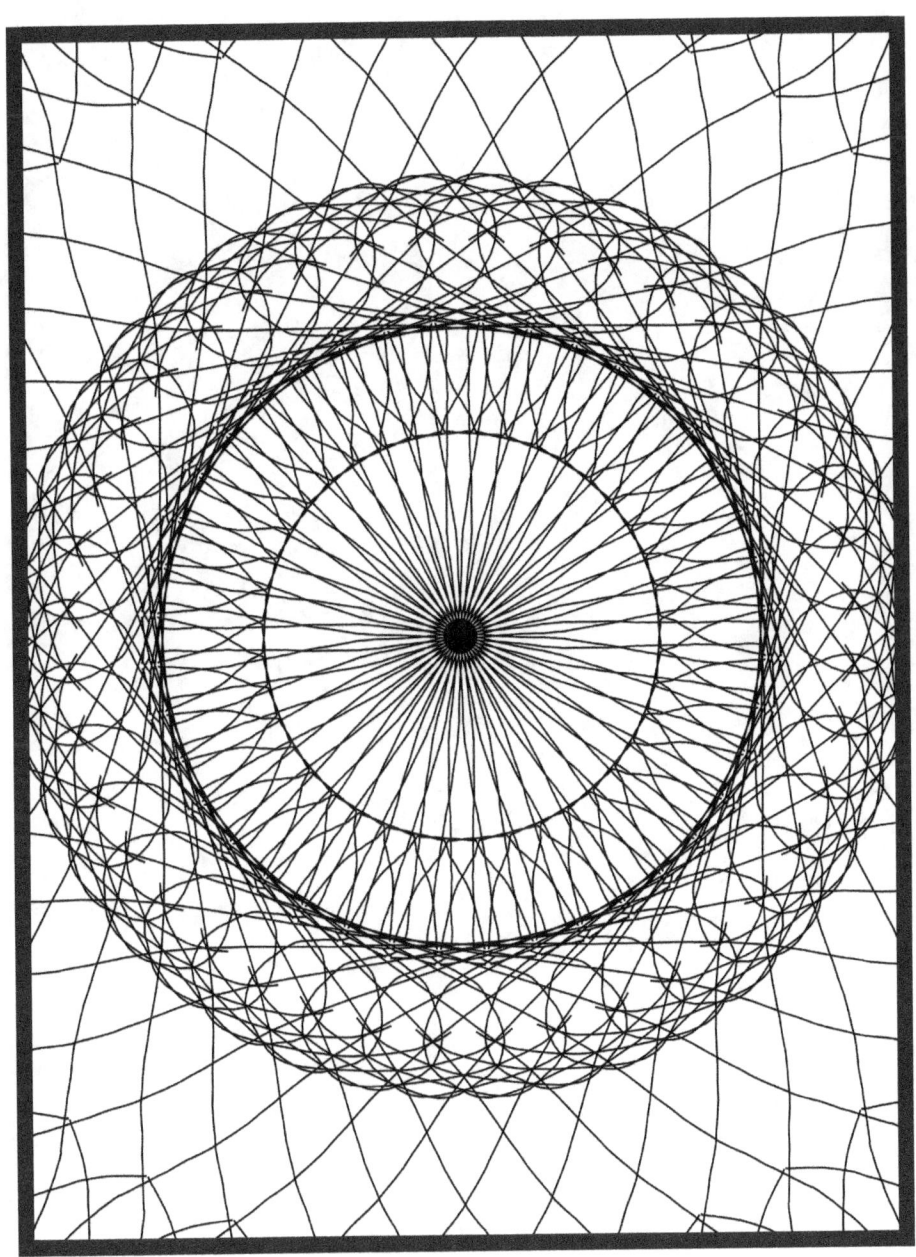

"Be a positive energy trampoline – absorb what you need and rebound more back." — Dave Carolan

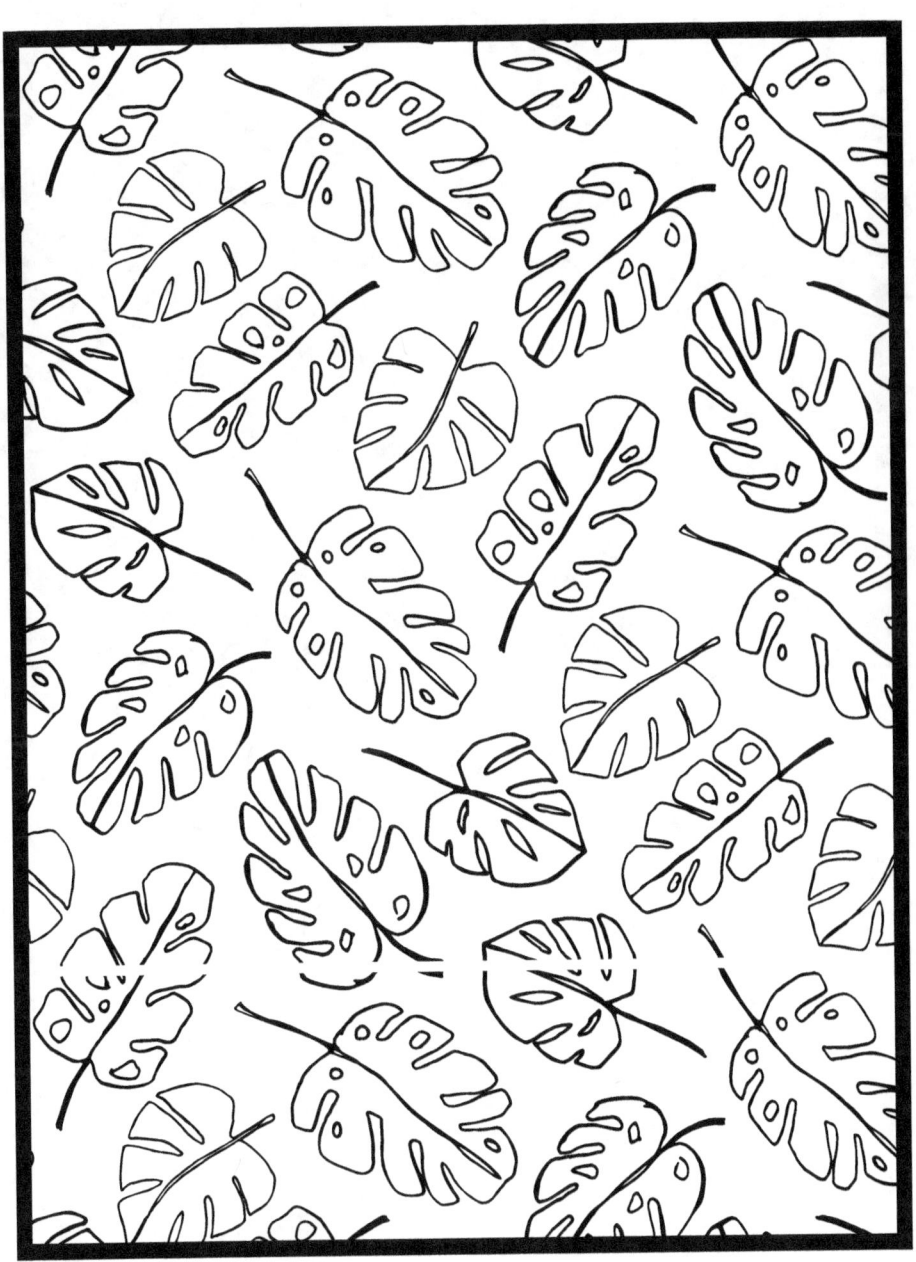

"People often say that motivation doesn't last. Well, neither does bathing – that's why we recommend it daily." — Zig Ziglar

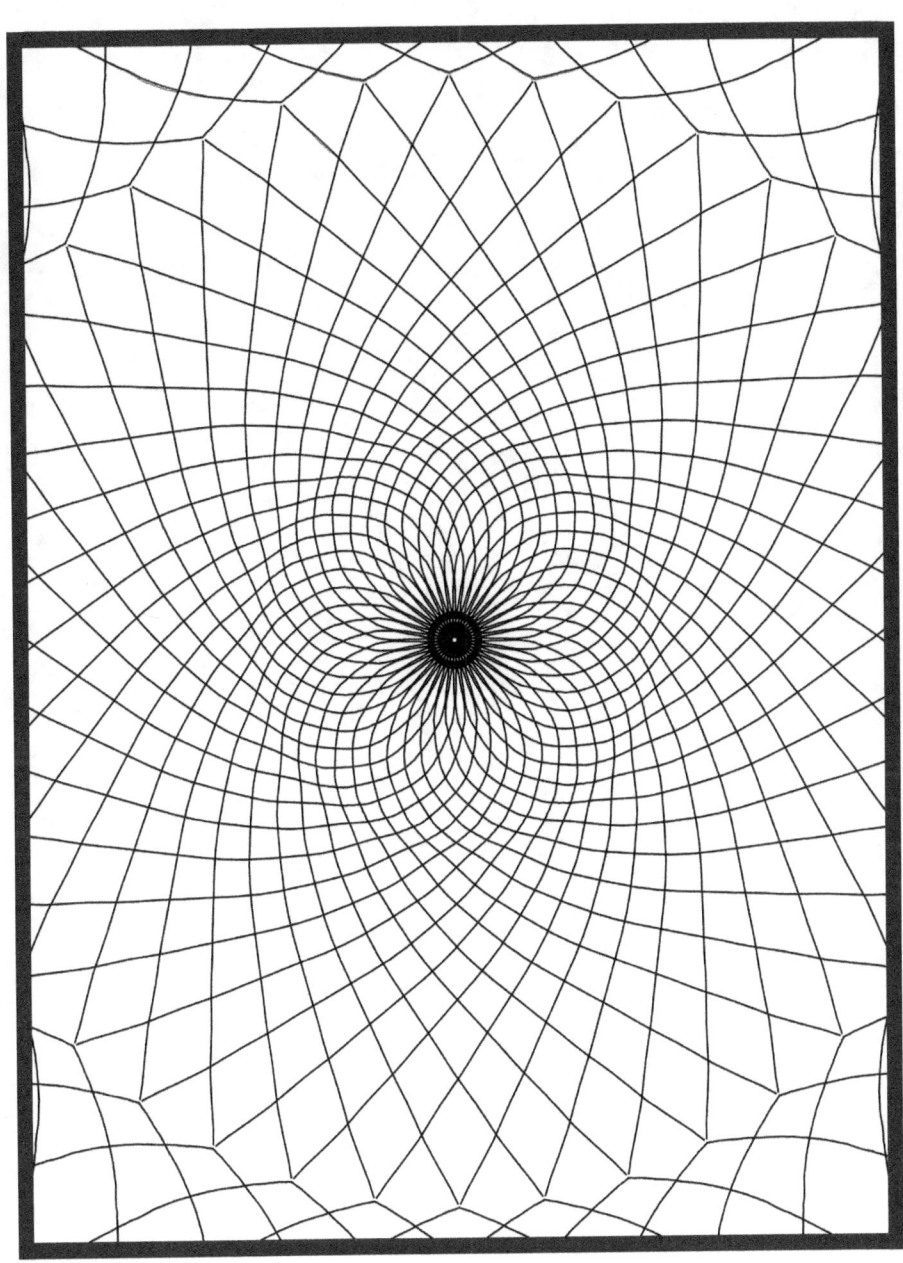

"Work until your bank account looks like a phone number." — Unknown

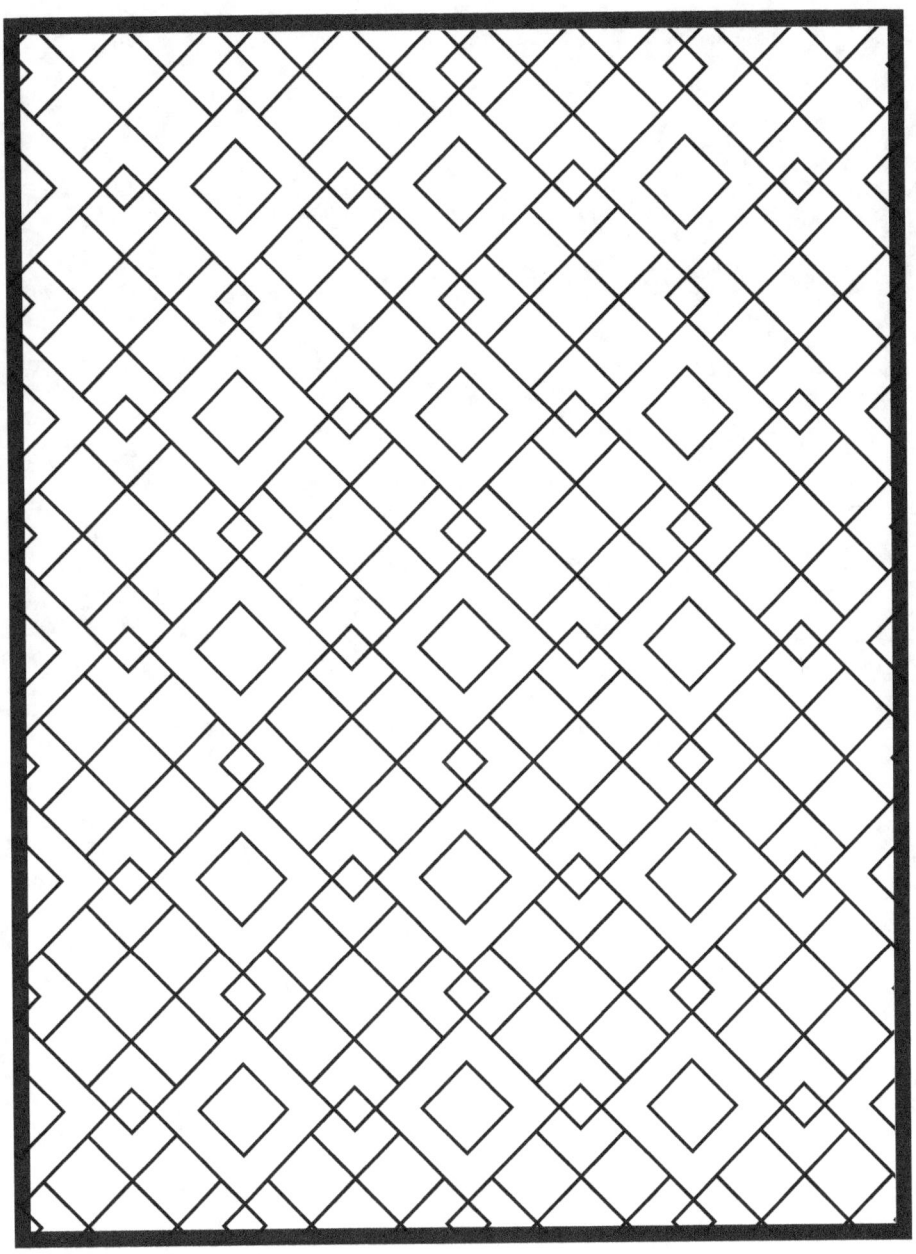

"I am so clever that sometimes I don't understand a single word of what I am saying." — Oscar Wilde

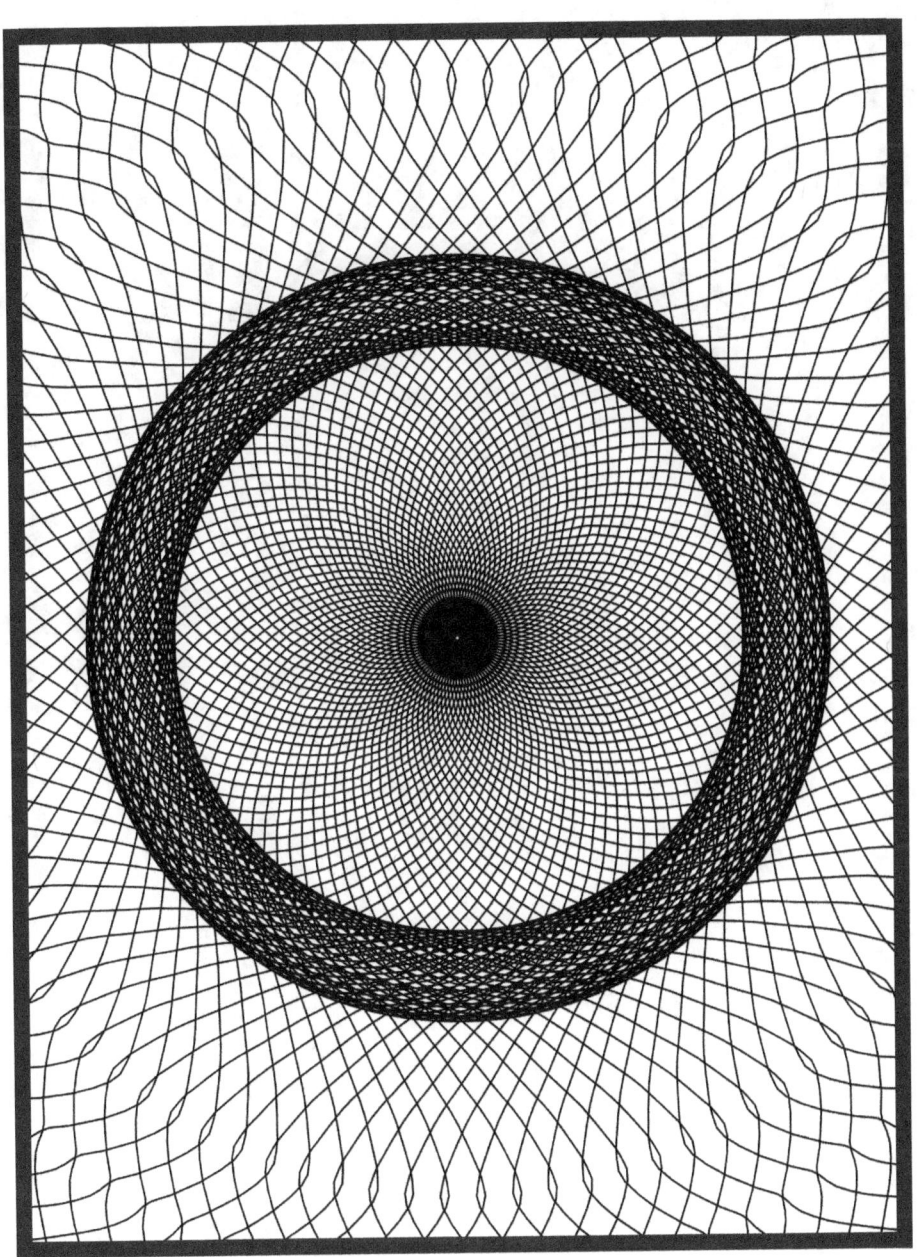

"People say nothing is impossible, but I do nothing every day." — Winnie the Pooh

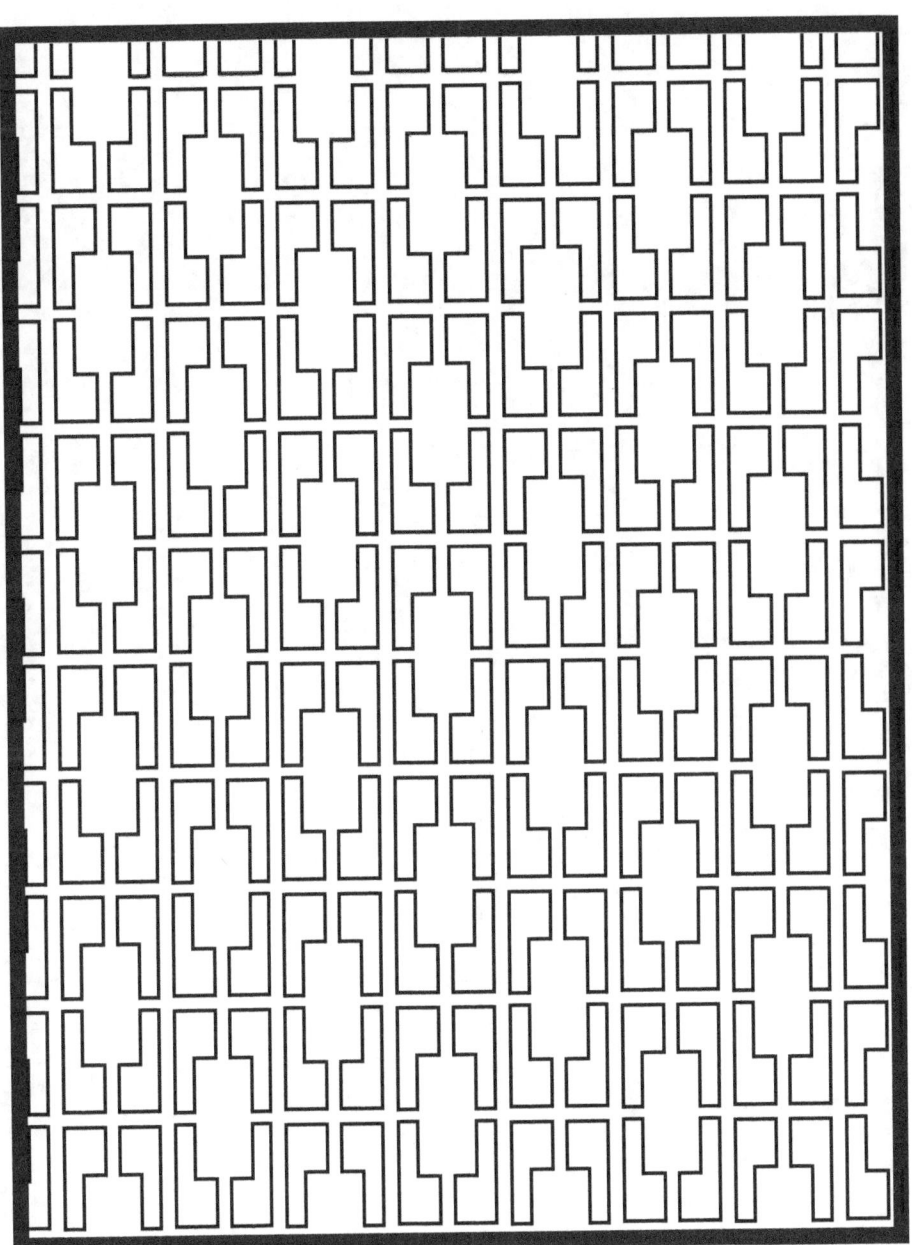

"Life is like a sewer... what you get out of it depends on what you put into it." — Tom Lehrer

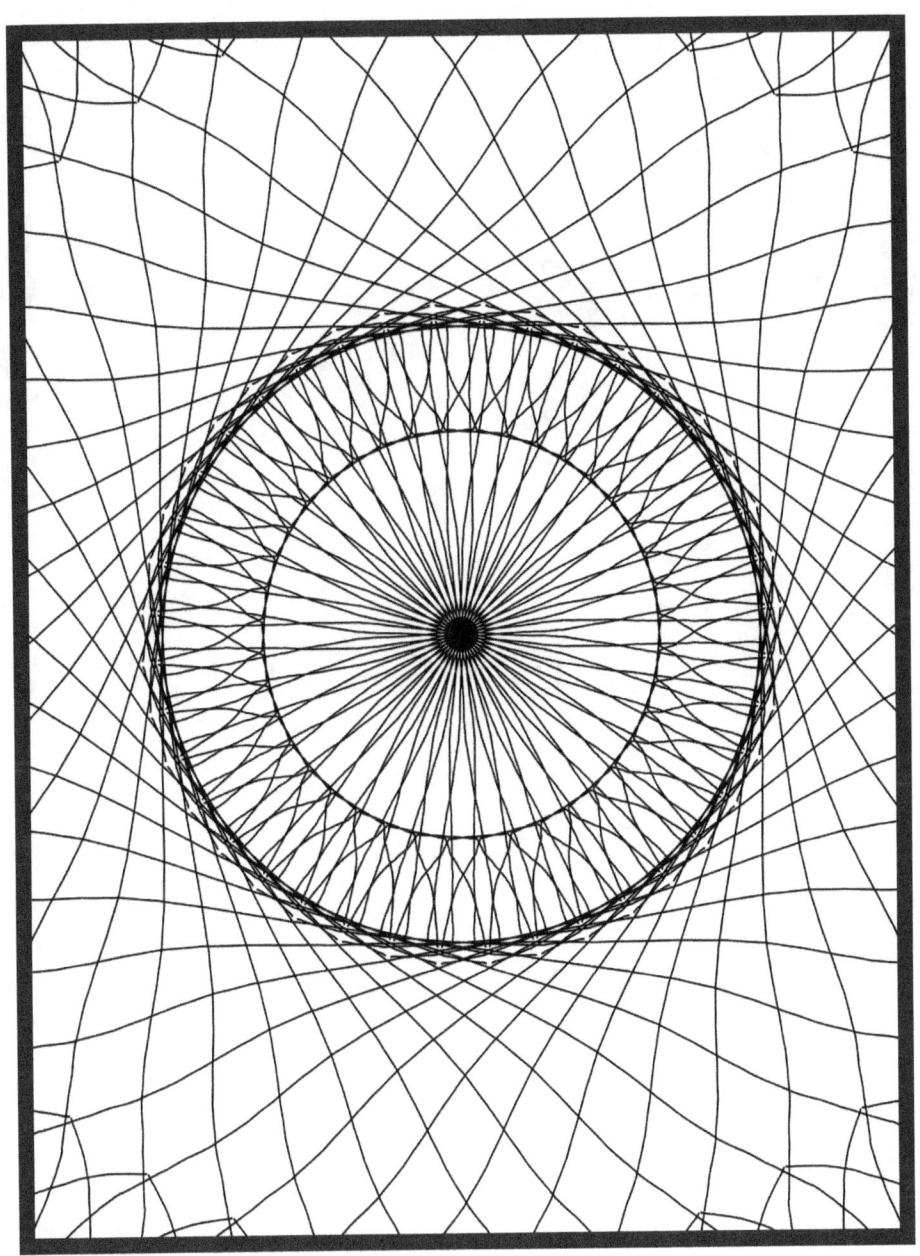

"I always wanted to be somebody, but now I realize I should have been more specific." — Lily Tomlin

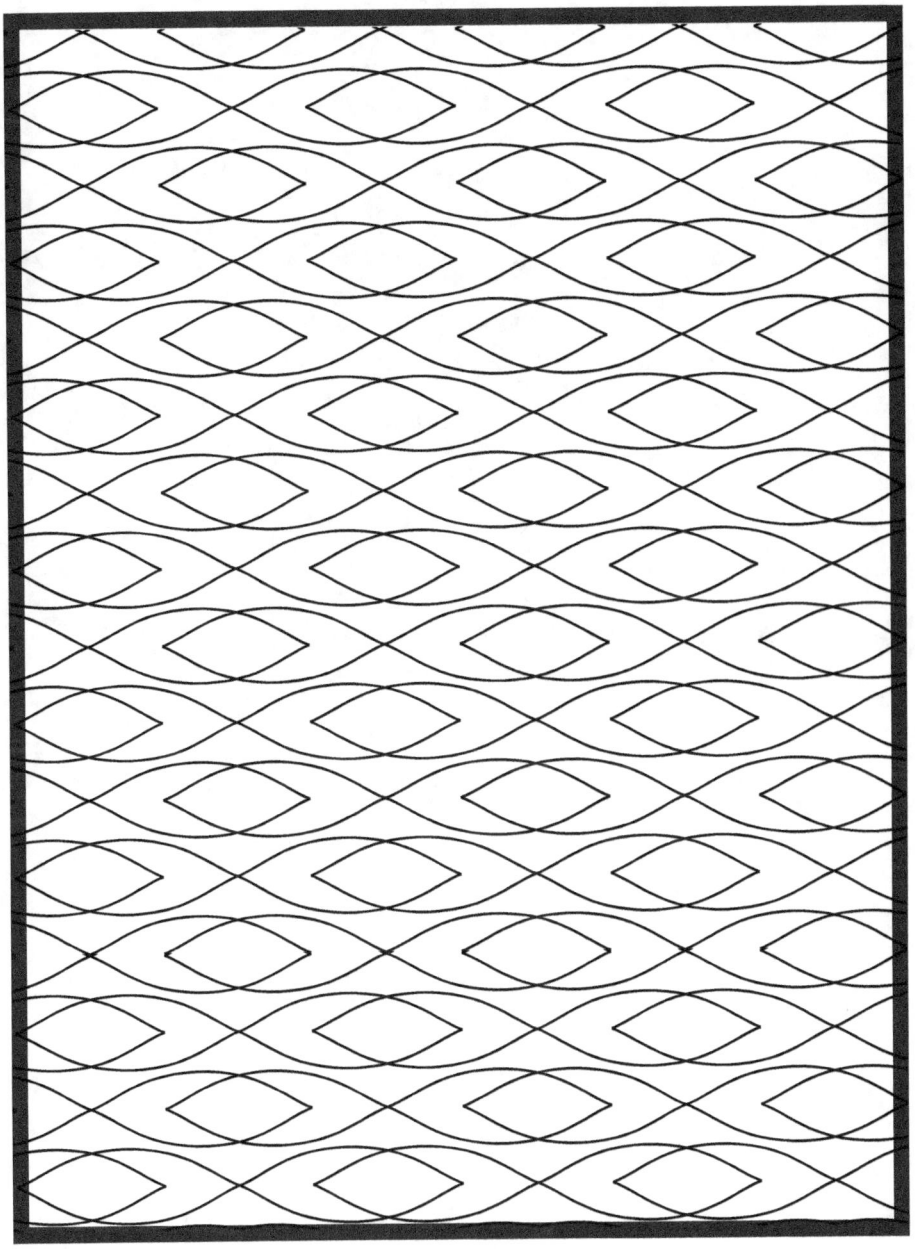

"Just one small positive thought in the morning can change your whole day." — Dalai Lama

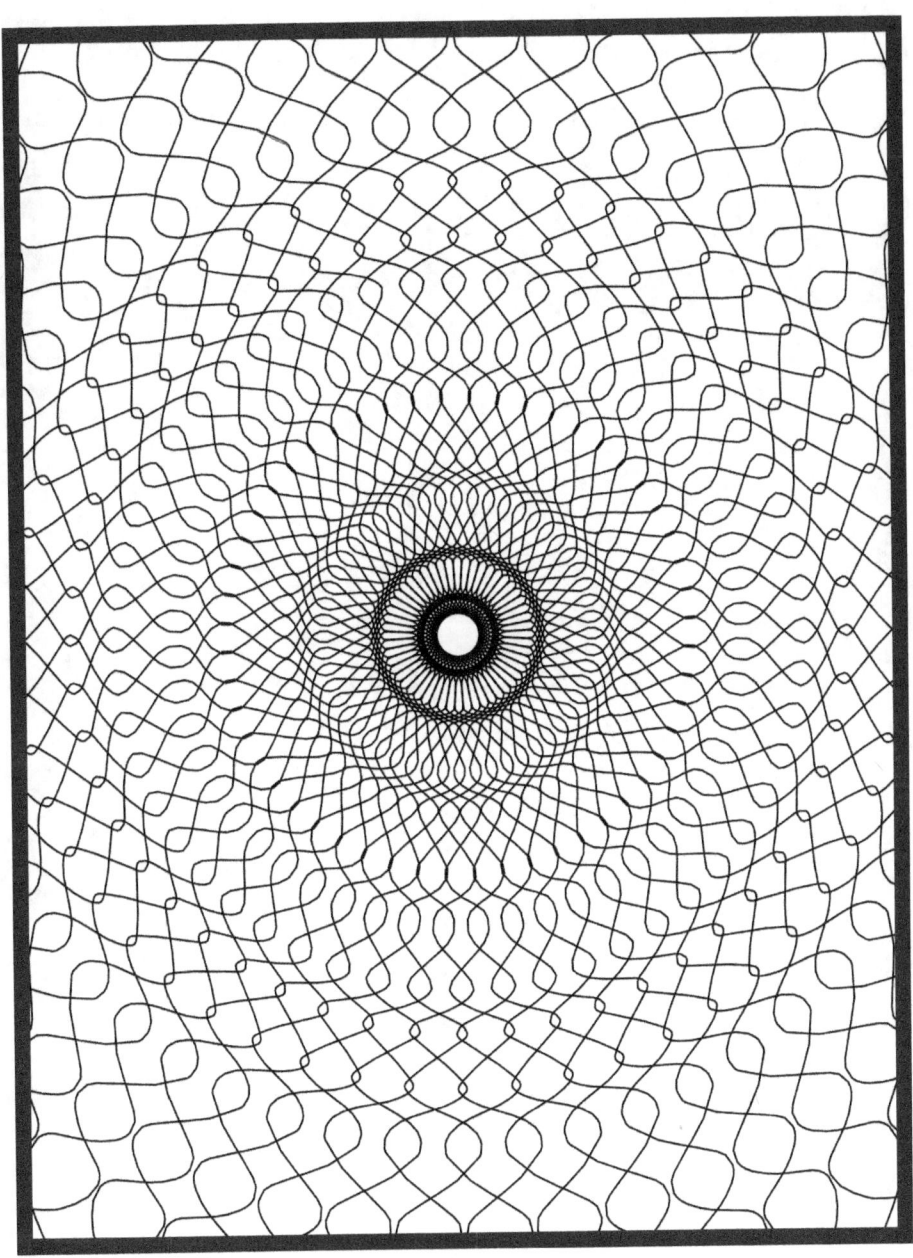

"Opportunities don't happen, you create them." — Chris Grosser

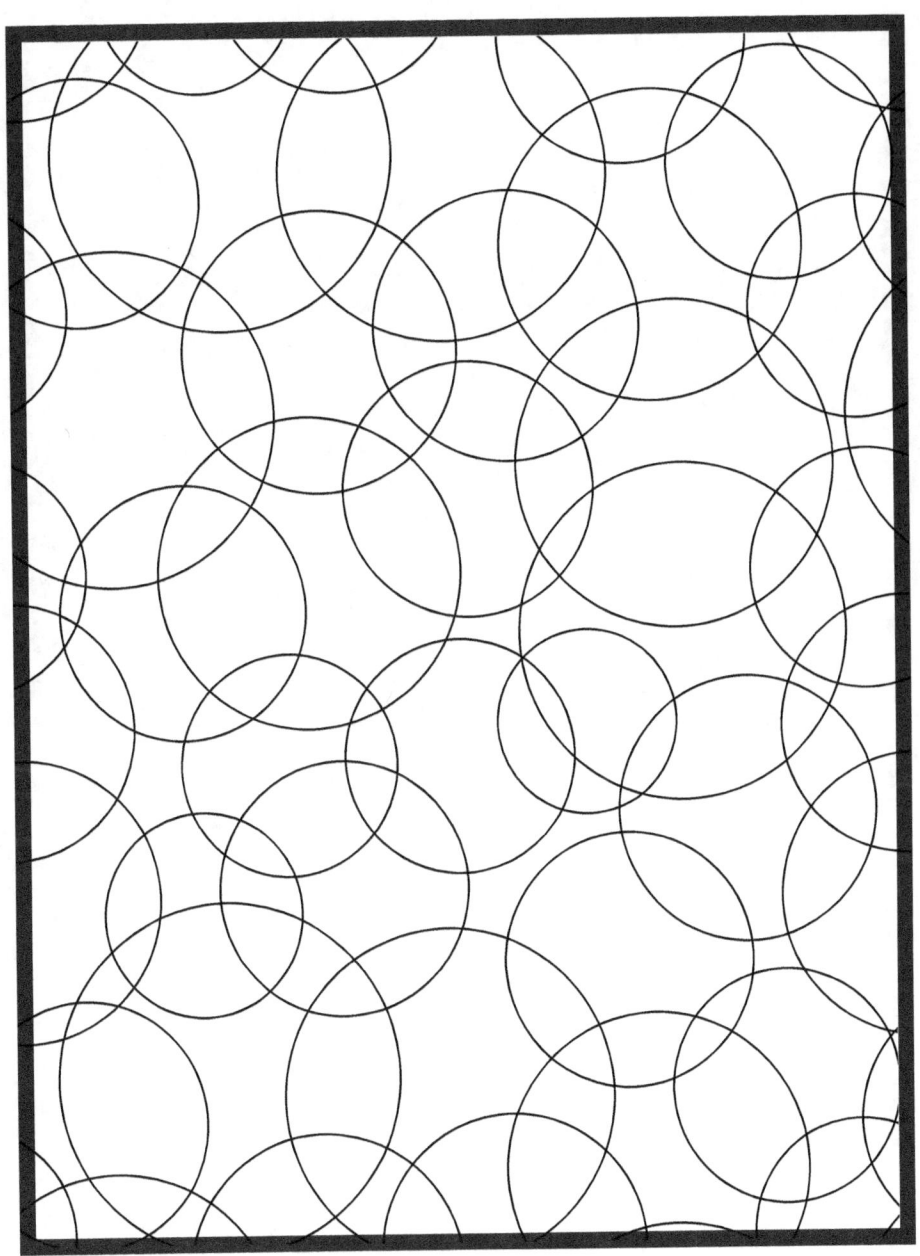

"Love your family, work super hard, live your passion." — Gary Vaynerchuk

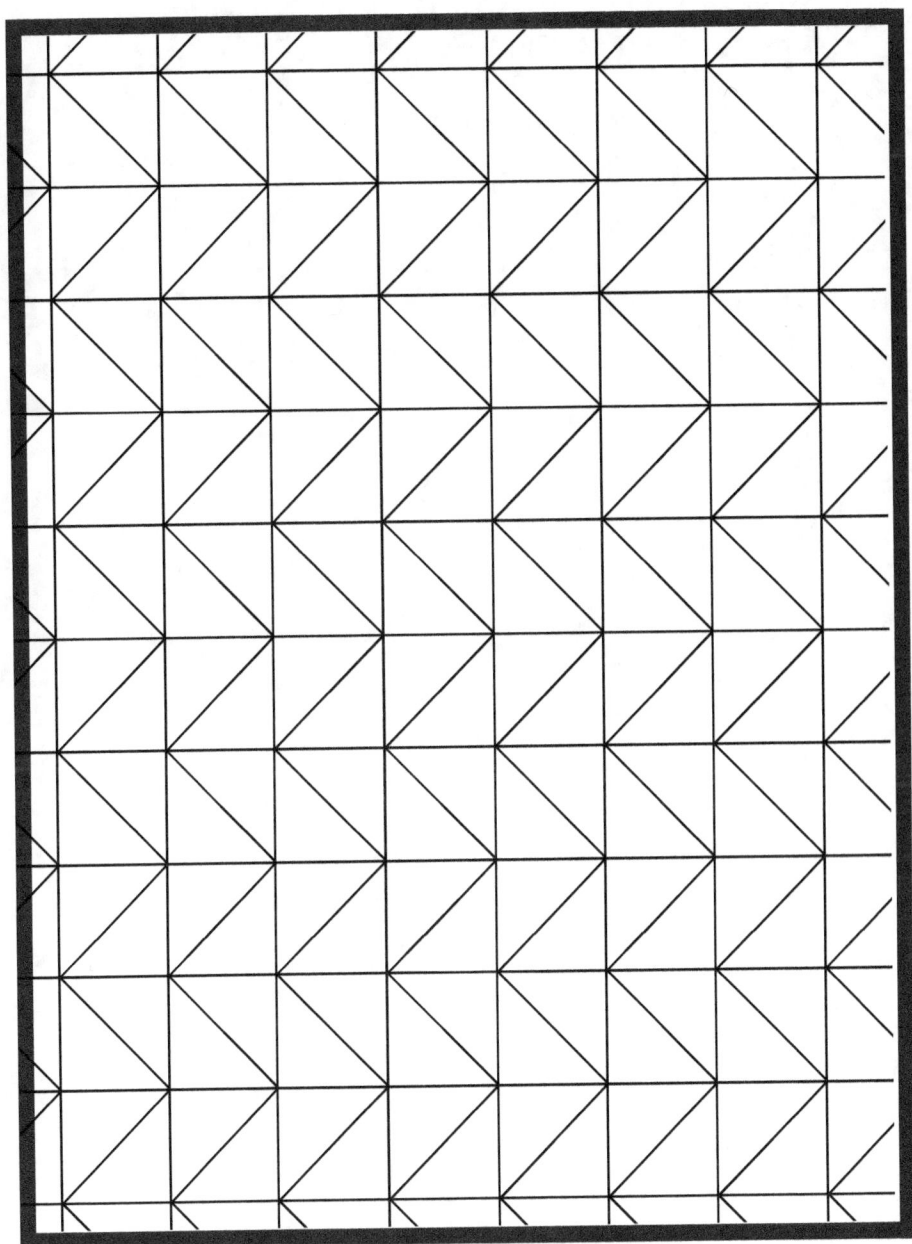

"It is never too late to be what you might have been." — George Eliot

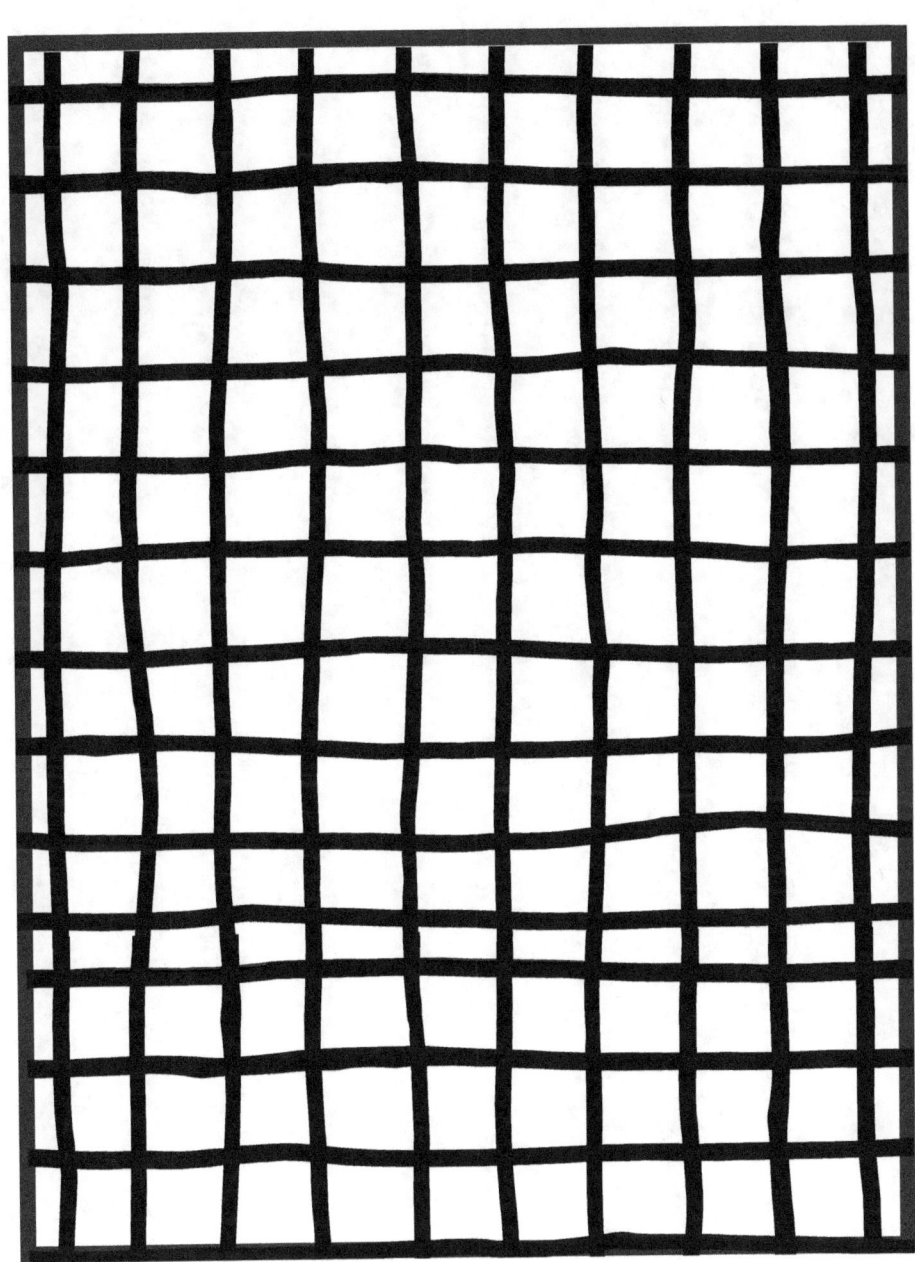

"Don't let someone else's opinion of you become your reality" — Les Brown

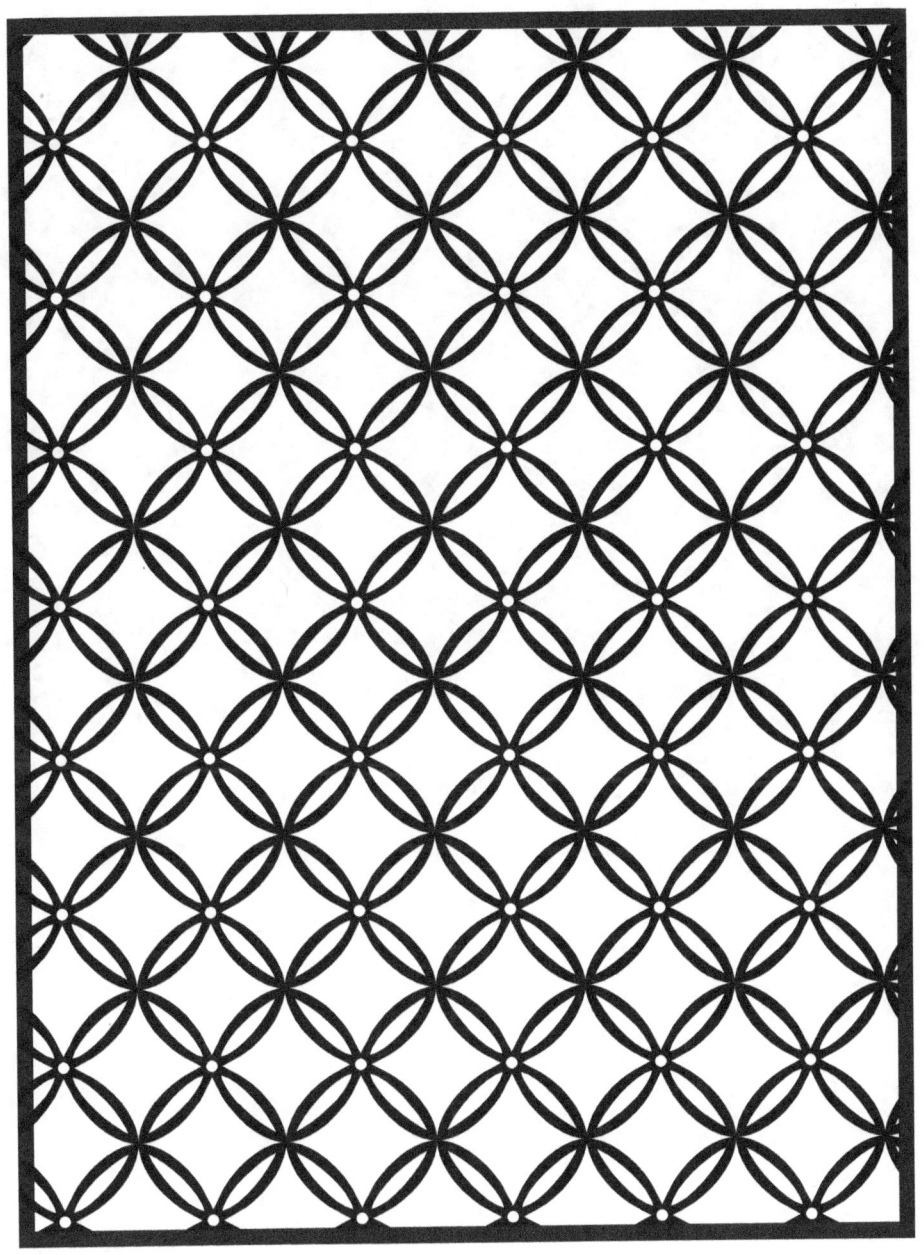

"If you're not positive energy, you're negative energy." Mark Cuban

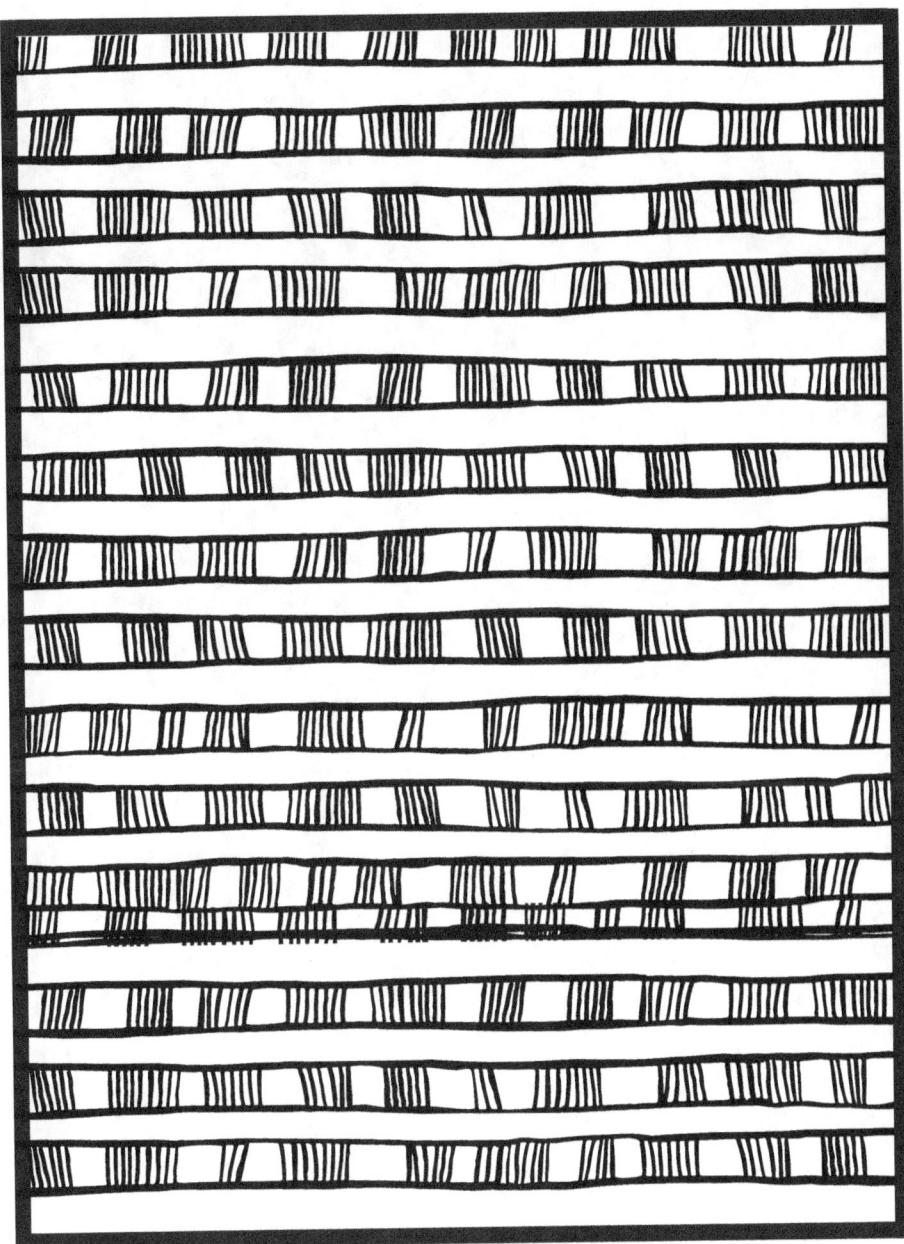

"I am not a product of my circumstances. I am a product of my decisions." — Stephen R. Covey

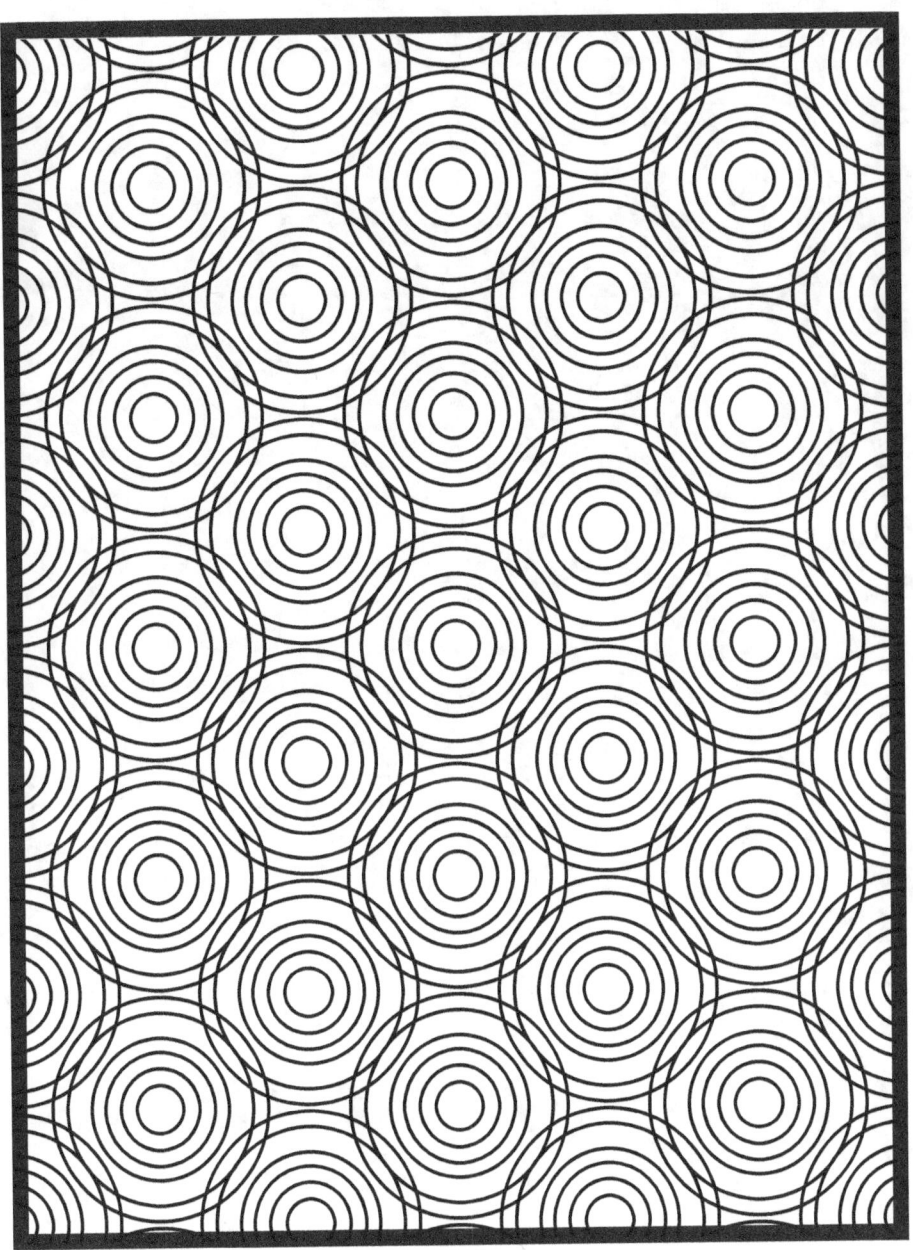

"You can get everything in life you want if you will just help enough other people get what they want." —Zig Ziglar

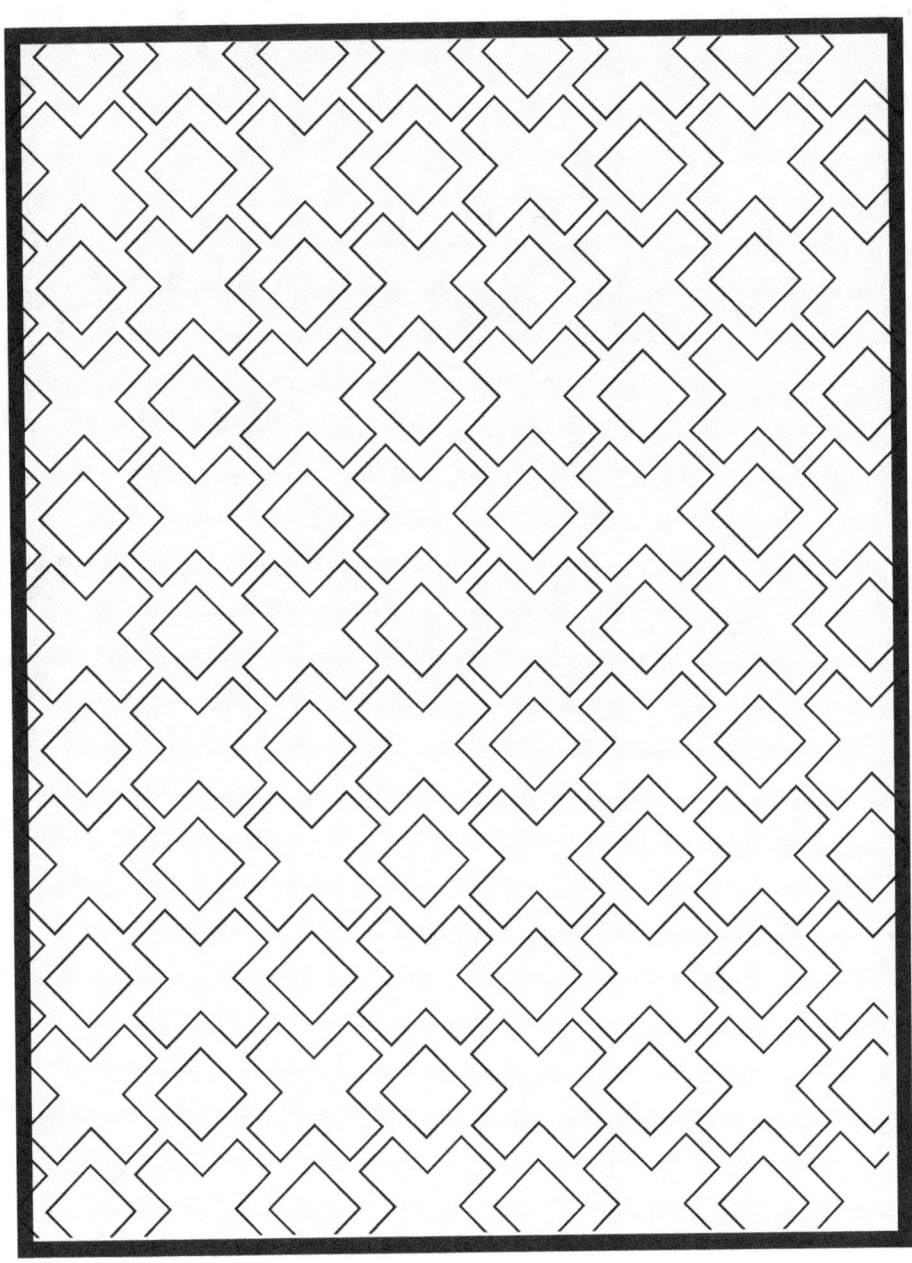

"Inspiration does exist, but it must find you working." —Pablo Picasso

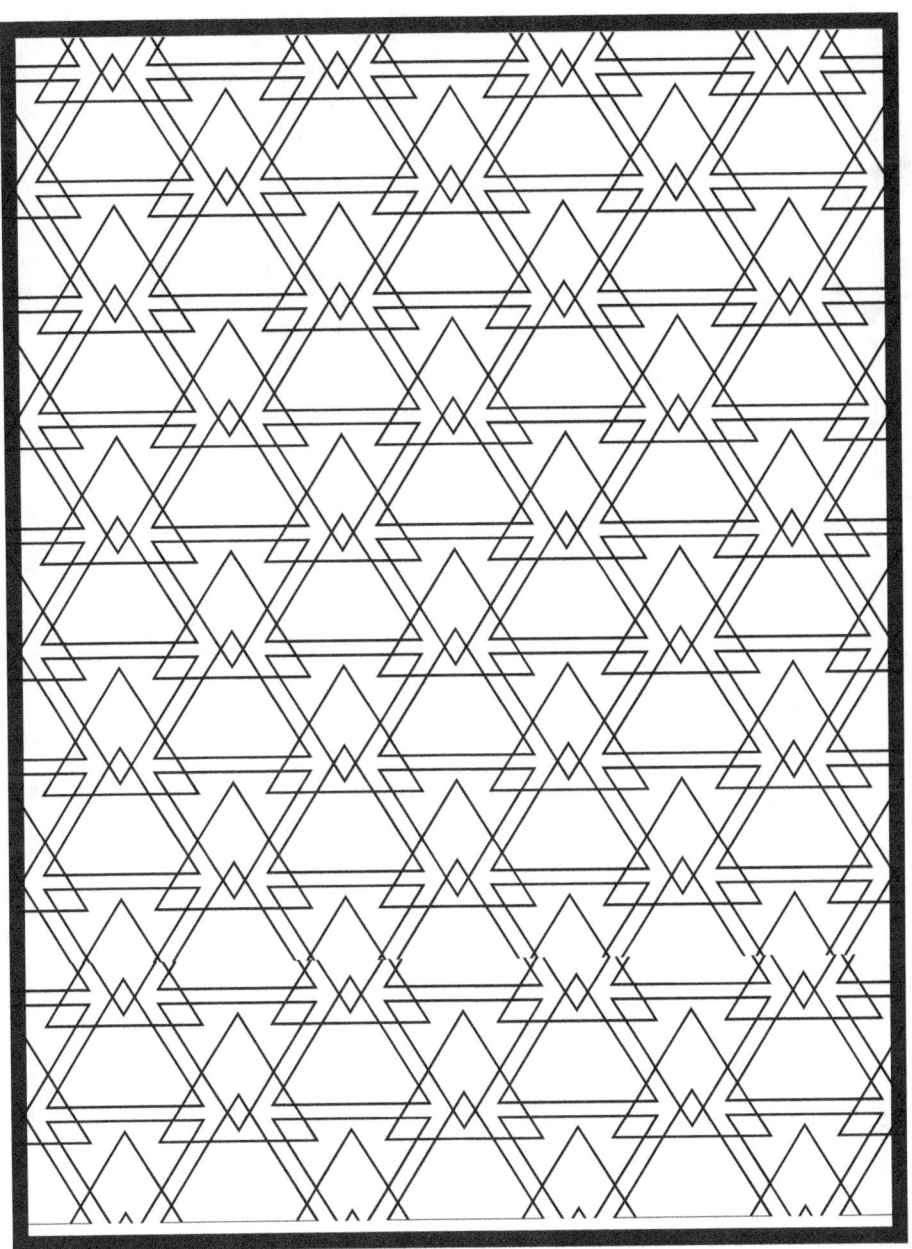

"Don't settle for average. Bring your best to the moment. Then, whether it fails or succeeds, at least you know you gave all you had." —Angela Bassett

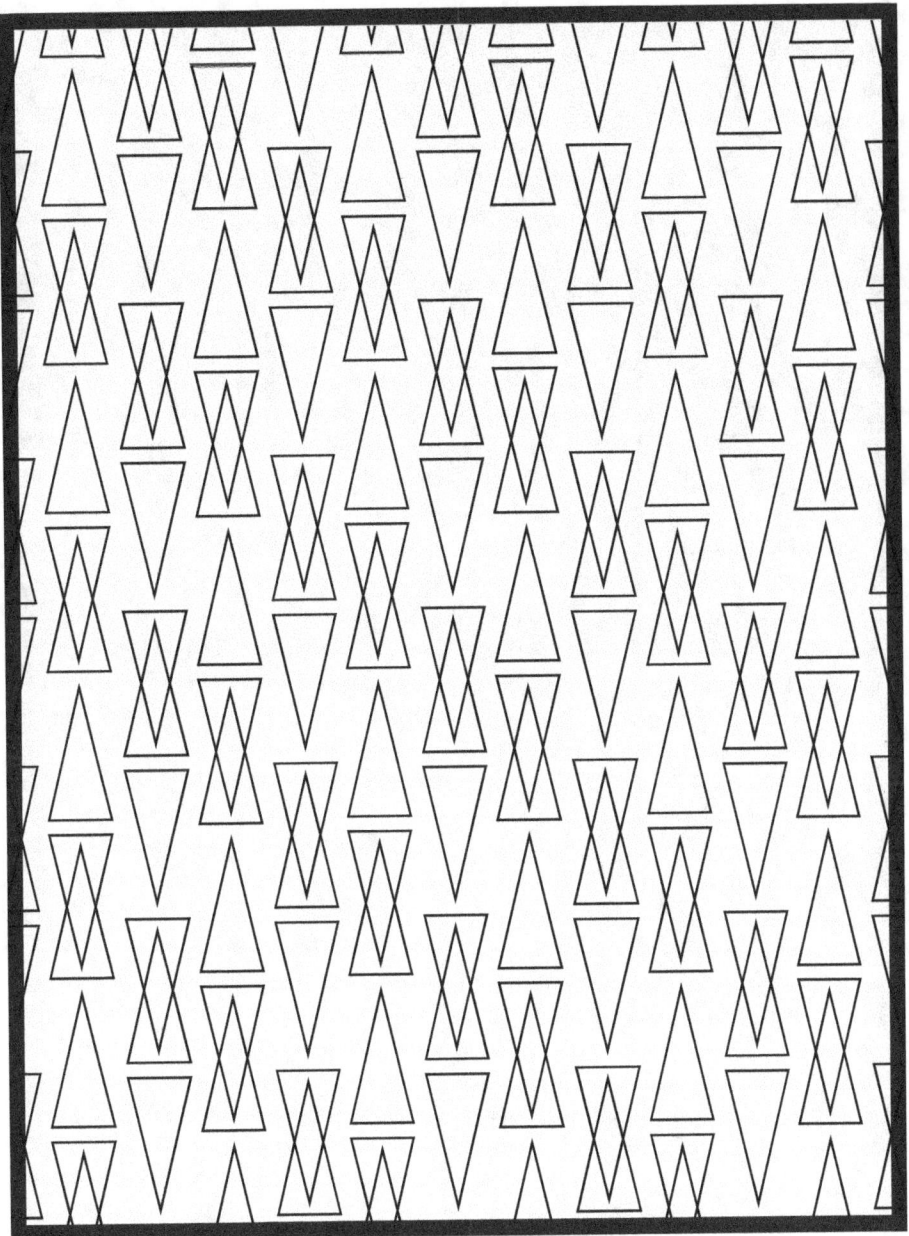

"Show up, show up, show up, and after a while the muse shows up, too." —Isabel Allende

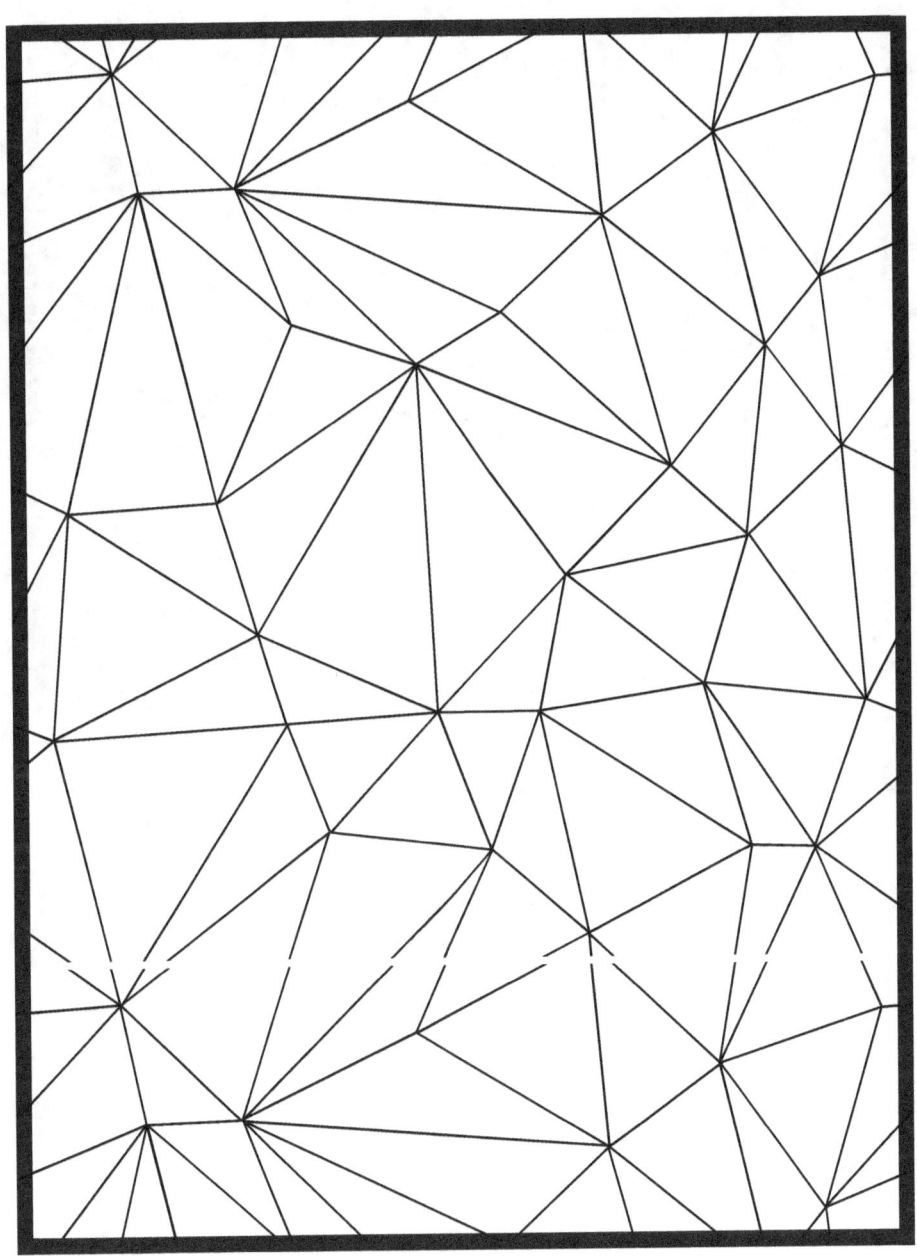

"Don't bunt. Aim out of the ballpark. Aim for the company of immortals." —David Ogilvy

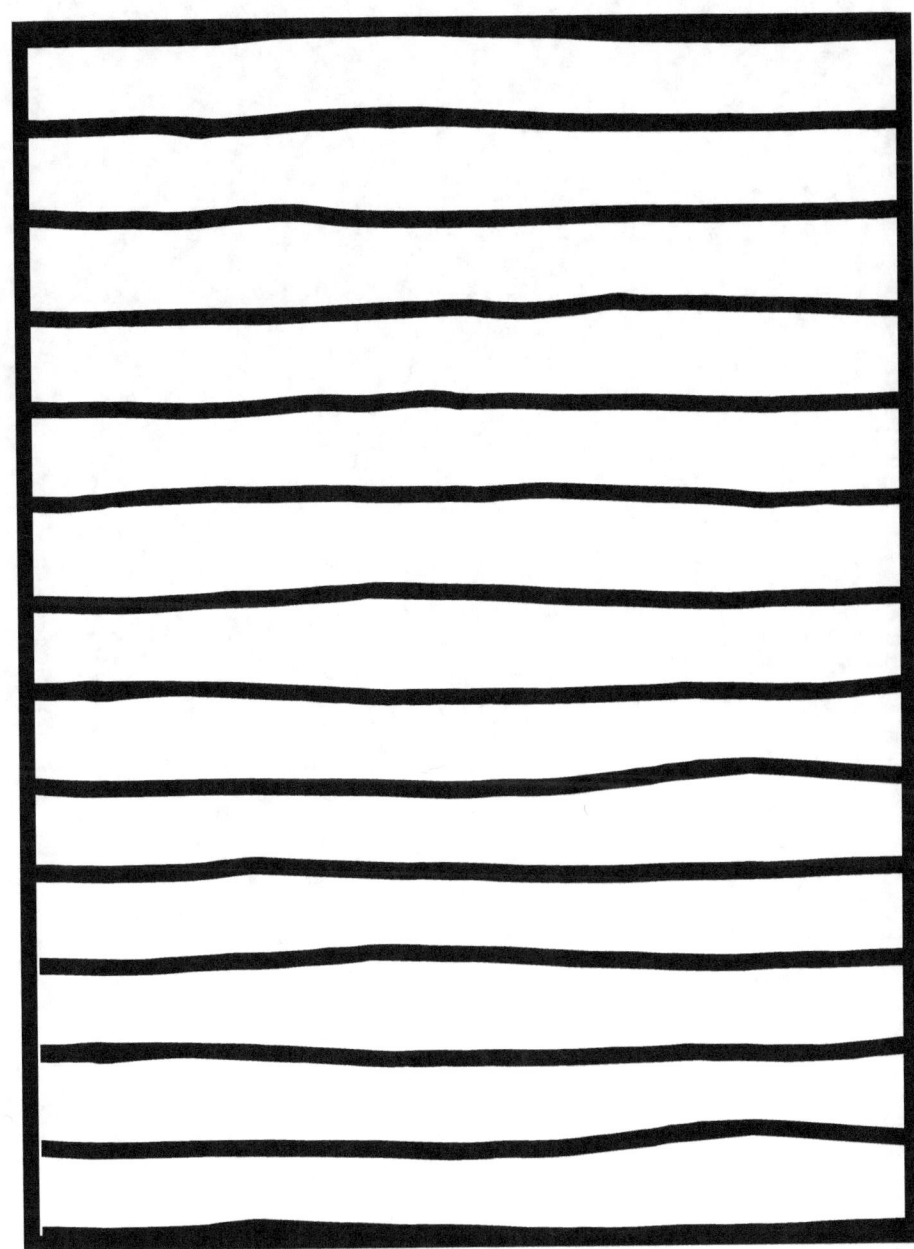

"I have stood on a mountain of no's for one yes." —Barbara Elaine Smith

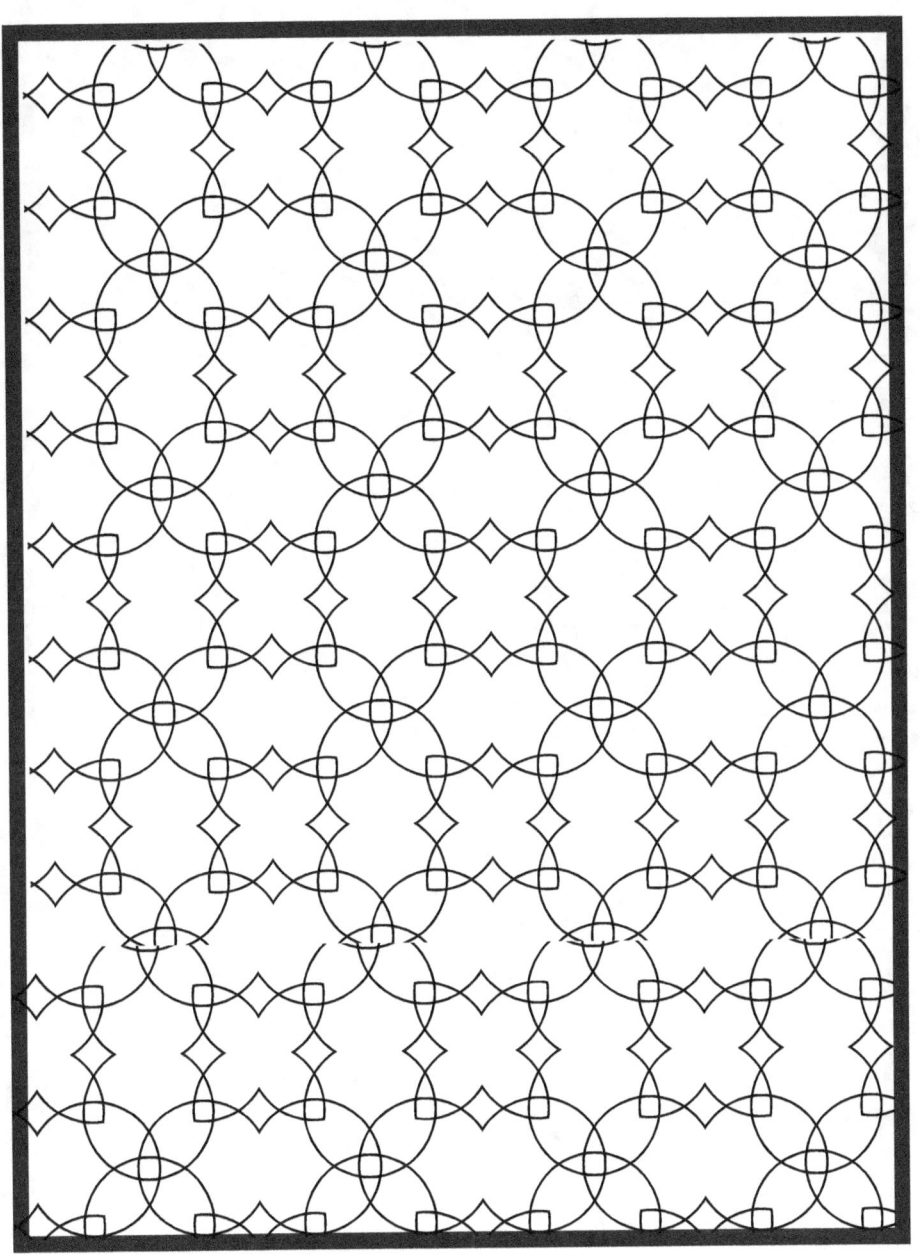

"If you believe something needs to exist, if it's something you want to use yourself, don't let anyone ever stop you from doing it." —Tobias Lütke

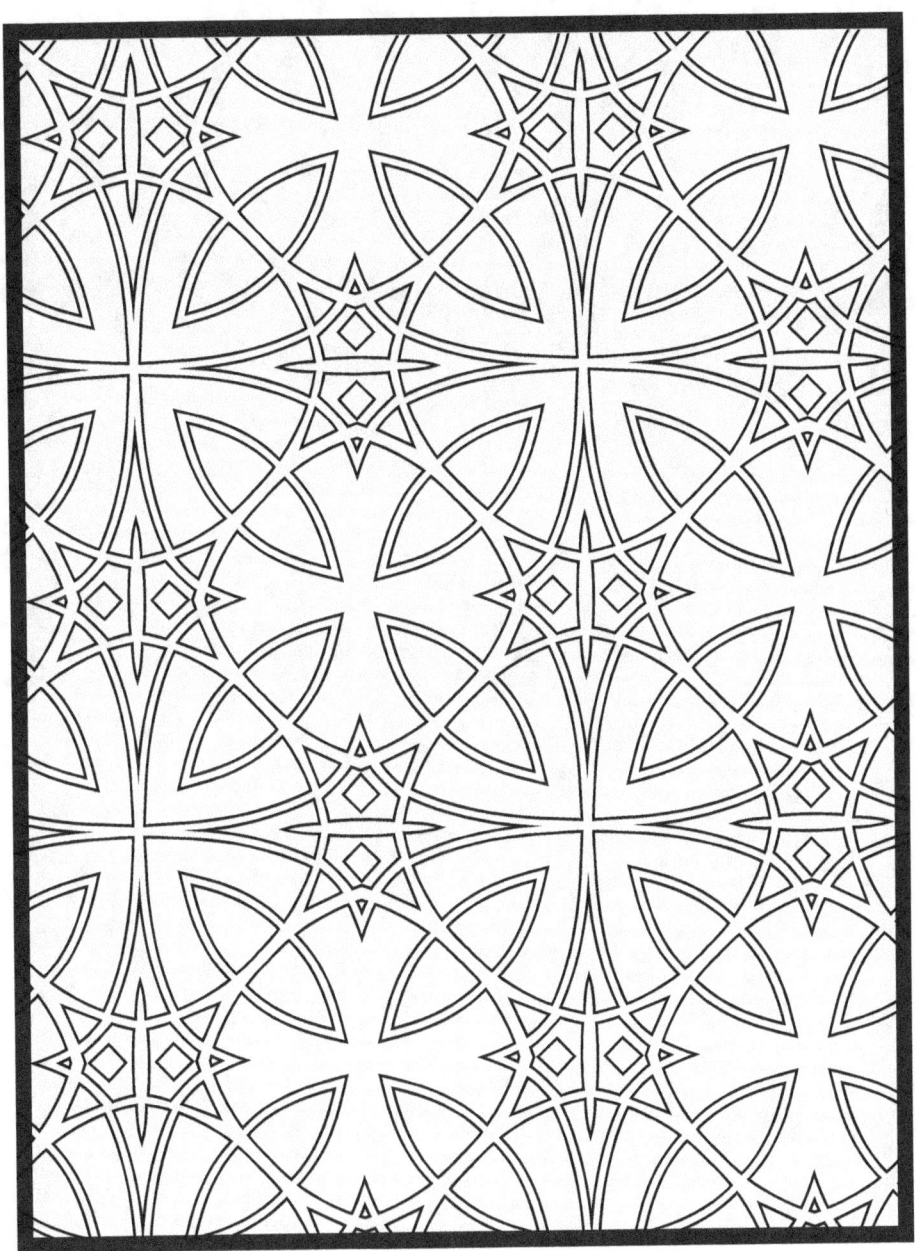

"Don't look at your feet to see if you are doing it right. Just dance." —Anne Lamott

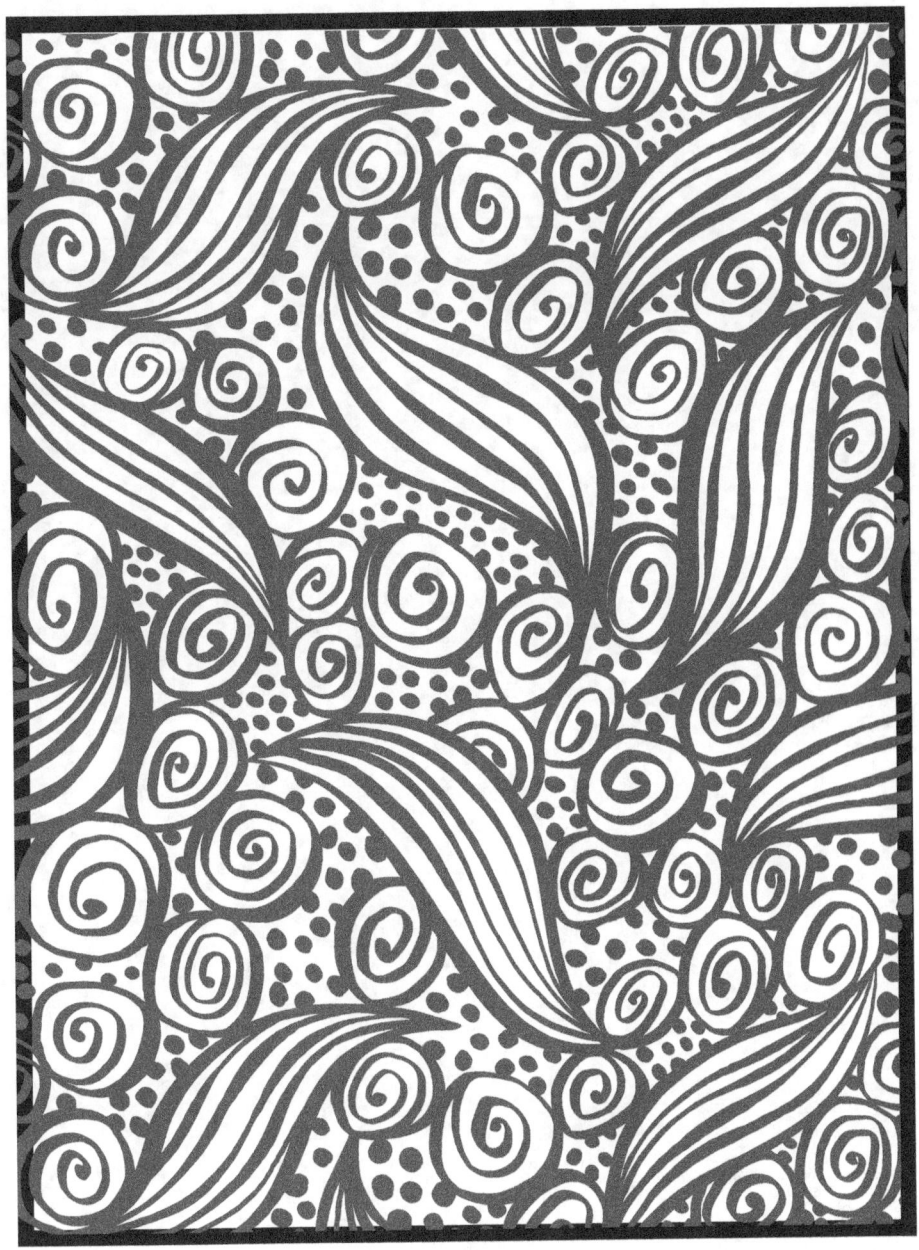

www.ingramcontent.com/pod-product-compliance
Lightning Source LLC
Chambersburg PA
CBHW070427240526
45472CB00020B/1514